Welcome To Teaching... And Our Schools

Robert L. DeBruyn
Author of *The MASTER Teacher*

The MASTER Teacher, Inc.
Publisher
Manhattan, Kansas
U.S.A.

THE MASTER TEACHER, INC.
Publisher
Leadership Lane
P.O. Box 1207
Manhattan, Kansas 66505-1207
Phone (800) 669-9633   Fax (800) 669-1132
www.masterteacher.com

ISBN 0-914607-49-9
First Printing 1997
Printed in the United States of America

TABLE OF CONTENTS

INTRODUCTION

This is the beginning of your teaching career in this district. The way you begin will influence your professional future. We're glad you're here, and we wish you the best. We want to help ensure your good beginning, one that will lead to immediate and future success, just as we're sure you want to help students have the kind of beginning this year that will give them immediate and future success.

The first days of school have special significance because people remember the firsts in their lives. Both research and experience indicate that beginnings are a significant factor in the formation of lasting opinions and attitudes. *Firsts* are the things of which impressions, images, and memories are made. Remember your first date? Remember your first car? First party? First childhood friend? Firsts are the milestones that people most often remember. That's why the first days in class will be the ones that linger in the minds of students.

As you begin the year, you must realize that students' reactions to learning and to school in general may be a reflection of teachers' attitudes. The entire school team must be prepared, in terms of attitude as well as subject matter, to be successful educators. We must be enthusiastically and willingly ready to meet the challenge of helping students win in school this year. If not, it will be a long, hard, and dull year for teachers and students alike.

Your future begins today. The future of your students begins today too—and you are responsible for both. You must lay the foundation for a successful future—for both yourself and your students—by presenting an image of yourself as a teacher who is a warm, friendly, caring human being, professionally competent to prepare young people for a better life. We wish you well. Your administrators are prepared to help you in any way possible. Their assistance is yours for the asking. The welfare of students is the fundamental concern of the entire school team. And you, as a teacher, are the vital element in the learning process. After all, it takes a quality teacher to give students a quality education. There is no research that supports anything to the contrary. If you're successful, students will be successful as well. On the other hand, if you fail, students will fail too.

CHAPTER

1

THE
FIVE
OBJECTIVES

If you are to be an effective teacher, your lesson plans must include more than just the academic subjects your students will study. They must also include the basic objectives of the whole schooling process. That's why, as professional educators, we all have a definite place to begin each school year—regardless of the grade or subject being taught. And we might all learn a valuable lesson regarding beginning from those teachers who meet students entering kindergarten for the first time.

When children begin their education in kindergarten, teachers know that meeting certain needs is paramount. That's why they begin with five objectives firmly in mind. These five objectives are essentials—whether you work with kindergartners or high school seniors. They are the basic ingredients of any teaching plan, no matter what grade or course you teach.

ASSURANCE AND OPPORTUNITY
FOR EACH AND EVERY STUDENT IN YOUR CLASS

The first objective is the recognition that all students need assurance that they are both liked and valued for themselves. This need has no age or grade boundaries—and can't be "ho-hummed" or "pooh-poohed" by any professional teacher.

Assurance of self-worth is the foundation for helping each student to fit into the school program, identify with learning, and strive to achieve to his or her potential. You begin to meet this need when you welcome students to your classes and tell them—individually and collectively—that you are glad they are there. Being warm, friendly, and enthusiastic on the first day is the way to begin reaching this objective. A cold and rigid approach is never the appropriate professional technique, regardless of any teacher reasoning that may appear to justify it.

On the first day, you need to share with students specifically what you have planned for them to achieve, rather than emphasize what they can't do—or what they are required to do. You can achieve this goal only by presenting yourself as a caring and helping partner in the learning process. If "making sure every student knows I'm the boss" is your first-day objective, you only lay the groundwork for student-teacher barriers, rather than for the openness and receptivity that you need so very much in order to be an effective and a happy teacher.

Second, your teaching plan must offer students *opportunities to learn by doing*, rather than simply by listening. Classroom and lesson plan structure is necessary, but so is a teaching plan that does not chain students to a desk in a formal stand-up, sit-down, raise-your-hand conformity. In meeting this objective you reveal your teaching creativity. Your lessons must stimulate activity and involvement for all, not just the eager and the bright. You must also extend to students the opportunity to try out their own ideas and develop self-expression.

Therefore, your teaching plan simply must provide your students with both an assurance of self-worth and an active role in learning. Herein lies a key to motivating students and making your teaching dynamic and relevant. This must be your starting point on the first day, as well as all the days that follow. In addition, you need to help students learn how to interact.

GIVING, TAKING, AND ACHIEVING: LESSONS FOR THE CLASSROOM—AND FOR LIFE

Third, students need *interaction with others* in order to learn how to give and take. This is a lesson they will use throughout life. None of us ever outgrow the need to find balance in life between giving and taking. That's why young people of all ages and all grades need to have the opportunity to work with others—directly.

A lesson plan that does not allow students interaction with both teacher and classmates leaves out a valuable asset necessary for productive living.

Fourth, students must develop *habits and attitudes that enable them to work at a task until it is completed.* They must learn to work amid distractions. The world doesn't stop or even slow down just to make it easier for people to get their jobs done. Students are not the exception to this reality of life. Interference and distractions are the norm in the classroom as well as in the world of work. That's why your lesson plan must be geared toward meeting students' need to acquire the self-discipline necessary to complete assignments and achieve goals. In many ways, the degree to which this objective is met determines whether or not students will be achievers—after graduation as well as while they are in school.

Finally, if you intend to meet these other four objectives, you cannot let your teaching plan become a rule rather than a tool. You must allow in your lesson plan the *flexibility to compensate for individual student needs, interests, abilities, and differences.* If you think all students can start at point A and arrive at point D just because this sequence is the structure of your course, class, or unit, you are mistaken. As professional educators, each of us must meet our students where they are academically and take them as far as they can go. That's what teaching is all about. Their starting points are our starting points.

YOU ARE THE VITAL ELEMENT
IN THE LEARNING PROCESS FOR ALL STUDENTS

The classroom teacher is the vital element in the learning process. A healthy student-teacher relationship is one of partnership. That's why you must not minimize the importance of the first days of school. Your beginning approach and plan convey the tone and may even establish the climate in the classroom for the entire year.

Never forget, fundamental educational objectives and philosophies don't vary with grade or age. Only the content of academic material and the level of sophistication progress with grade and age. Your lesson plans must be focused on the individual student. You do not teach a class. You teach students in a class. The student rather than the subject matter is the first consideration.

Realizing this truth will keep your professional perspective intact and allow you to approach your responsibilities from a student-centered viewpoint.

If you give all students the opportunity to meet their needs through these five objectives, you will have given them an educational experience that will provide them with a lifetime of benefits. The master teacher realizes that the challenge and the expertise of teaching are to make the journey of learning as exciting and rewarding as the satisfaction of reaching the destination. You can never forget this truth if you want to be successful in the classroom. In addition, you must be aware of the relationships all students have in the classroom.

CHAPTER
2

THE FIVE RELATIONSHIPS OF STUDENTS

Development of mental health for a child in the school setting is, without doubt, primarily the result of five relationships:

- The student and himself/herself
- The student and the teacher
- The student and peers
- The student and school curriculum /activities
- The student and the home

As the primary agent in the development and fulfillment of these relationships, you can never forget—even for a moment—that the individual student is the common element in all of them. Too, these relationships cannot be separated, for they are interrelated— and this interrelationship must be the focus of your approach. The real question is this: How can you relate to students as they function within these five relationships?

THE FIRST RELATIONSHIP: THE STUDENT AND HIMSELF/HERSELF

First, you can best begin helping children by accepting them rather than writing them off because of behavior, level of ability or achievement, or personality. Too often, we size up children quickly on the first day of school. "I've got his number," we say.

Impossible! When we do this, we have stepped out of the arena of diagnostician to become judges. This is a professional mistake that has serious repercussions for teacher and child alike.

Never forget that when students come to the classroom, they've been thinking for five to eighteen years about who they are, what they are, and what they want to be or don't want to be. Your role as a teacher is not just to view students as you see them yourself. You must also view them as they see themselves. This is the key to understanding behavior. It is the only professional position that allows a teacher to detect truth and react appropriately in agreement with our professional responsibility to pick children up academically *wherever they are* and take them as far as they can go.

When we size up students and then proceed, we usually proceed in the wrong direction. Failure to view children as they see themselves causes teachers to put children in positions, within each of the five relationships, that they can't deal with. The more drastic example of this mistake is the student who displays a change in behavior that shocks us. How many times have you heard someone say, "Joan was such a nice girl. She had everything going for her. I just can't understand what happened"? One thing happened for sure: Somebody did not see Joan as she saw herself. Had someone been alert enough to recognize how Joan felt about herself, maybe "what happened" wouldn't have happened.

There are students sitting in your classroom about whom you may know very little. Find out how they view themselves. Then, and only then, can individualized instruction have any real meaning in your classroom.

THE SECOND RELATIONSHIP: THE STUDENT AND THE TEACHER

You must continually elevate students' thinking regarding the student-teacher relationship. Many teachers' thoughts include "How can I get along with students, and how can students get along with me?" Too often, however, the emphasis is on the latter.

Never overlook the fact that students do not necessarily come to class liking the teacher or vice versa. But all students do enter class looking for help—consciously or subconsciously. Your responsibility is to give it. The vast majority of students enter the classroom *hoping or wishing* for a good year, or a better year than last. If you can't give students hope, then hopelessness will soon be their condition. Then, your troubles will begin.

A close look will reveal that problems for teachers come when, for one reason or another, they choose to deny help. And there are many ways to deny a child the student-teacher relationship necessary for sound mental health as well as academic achievement. We may deny students this relationship by what we do—or what we don't do. Actions such as ignoring their questions, belittling their values, failing to keep appointments with them, or classifying their interests as trivial communicate that we don't care about them as people. You need only review your class roster name by name to see how you are affecting the student-teacher relationship of each child entrusted to your care.

THE THIRD RELATIONSHIP: THE STUDENT AND SCHOOL CURRICULUM/ACTIVITIES

This is the student relationship you may know best. Yet, you may often think in terms of the class and the curriculum rather than of the student and the curriculum. Without doubt, the curriculum places some students in an impossible situation. This is most obvious on the secondary level. Math, for instance, may be an overwhelmingly difficult experience for some students, but they know they cannot graduate without it. Therefore, they struggle, often against almost insurmountable odds, and become more and more frustrated when no provision is made for them as individuals within the curriculum.

If you have difficulty accepting the need for flexible in-class requirements, take a good look at some of the students in your school who are regarded as failures. You'll find that at some point most of these students excelled in some areas and with some teachers. Yet, if you trace their school history, you can often find a curriculum problem that caused a whole chain of events producing school trouble.

You must always be aware of the academic relationship in a child's life. The relationship of the student and the curriculum can be the problem. Likewise, lack of success in extra-class activities in the school may lie at the root of the difficulty. Once this is detected, class requirements which are flexible or extra-class activities which fill each student's needs—coupled with your approach and attitude—can provide these students with fulfillment rather than frustration.

THE FOURTH RELATIONSHIP:
THE STUDENT AND PEERS

In some way or another and to varying degrees, everybody needs somebody. The child who cannot relate to his or her peers may be in trouble in the school setting. It's easy to see why. Most teachers become familiar very quickly with the extremes of students who have peer relationship problems. Yet, it's important not to overlook the vast majority who seem well-adjusted. Too often, we recognize the personality deficiencies of students who have extreme problems, but fail to discover whether the needs of the vast majority of our students are being met. Yet, we hold some responsibility for the peer relationships of these students, too.

There is much we can do to help a student fulfill the need for peer relationships. We deny such help most often, though, by our structure. The lecture situation does absolutely nothing to meet this need. Neither does the "stand up, sit down, raise your hand and I'll recognize you" teaching approach. Here, there is no opportunity at all for the student to develop any of the five needed relationships.

Remember, you are the primary instrument in the creation of good mental health in the classroom. And good mental health is, without reservation, vital in determining the well-being, satisfaction, and productivity of students—as well as in determining your success.

THE FIFTH RELATIONSHIP:
THE STUDENT AND THE HOME

When a child is having trouble, we must always look to a child's relationships at home. The questions are these: What are the conditions at home? Do parents pressure a child too much—or not at all? Are parents experiencing marital problems? Is the child abused? Is the family experiencing financial problems or health problems? When a child is having problems at home, the teacher

12

must make adjustments. If we don't, the child will continue having problems at school.

Remember, too, that all five relationships are interrelated and cannot be separated. In any situation, therefore, we cannot look at one relationship without also looking at the other four. In most cases that baffle us, one of three mistakes is being made. First, we "figure out" a student without looking at the child and his or her five relationships—individually. Second, we look at one facet without even being aware of the other four and their importance to each student. Finally, purposely or inadvertently, we deny students one or more of these relationships in our classroom. When we do any of these things, we have arrived at all our answers without asking the right questions. Then a failure of some kind becomes more than a possibility. It becomes the probability. And when students fail, we fail too—automatically. To aid student success, let's discuss a choice students don't have.

CHAPTER

3

A CHOICE
STUDENTS
DON'T HAVE

Without doubt, both students and teachers have some choices to make at the beginning of school. Students can choose to be "good" or "bad." They can decide to give their best effort, little effort, or no effort at all. They can even choose to get involved in class and school activities, or to remain detached. But there is one choice they don't have. It has to do with how good their teachers will be. That is up to us.

WE CHOOSE HOW GOOD WE WILL TRY TO BE

You—and you alone—determine what kind of teacher your students will have. Make no mistake regarding this truth. And you know right now how good a teacher you intend to be this year. All of us need to face this reality. If we have decided not to give a total effort, we can also choose to change our minds after looking at the possible consequences.

If striving for professional excellence is your choice, then you have decided to work both for students and for yourself. If you have not made such a decision, you may end up working against both. That's a fact. Your professional attitudes and your efforts toward excellence are really the only two things that guarantee your integrity in the classroom.

Remember, no student can decide whether you will strive to be a good teacher. And there is nothing that students can do about your choice, either. They are stuck. They can disobey, become discipline problems, or refuse to learn. But all these behaviors will work against them too.

As adults, we can choose doctors and lawyers. We can even choose our teachers. But young people in schools don't have these prerogatives. Worse, if we aren't good teachers, our students have but one choice: They can only endure us. And if they're smart, they will endure us without a word of criticism or displeasure. That's a lot of endurance. As teachers, we need to ponder the significance of this reality. After all, a classroom teacher has the power to decide how much effort will be put into his or her teaching every hour and day of the year.

SPECIFIC PRIORITIES ENHANCE YOUR PROBABILITY FOR SUCCESS

If you decide to be a good teacher, there are some things you need to do. You must order your priorities to enhance your probability for success. You can't spend more time on your expectations for students than on your preparation for teaching. That's why you can't make rules and regulations by the dozen— when one major one would do. For instance, instead of listing all the types of infractions, it would be far better to settle on one rule: People and property are to be treated with respect at all times.

This is open-ended, positive, and upbeat—rather than negative and restrictive. Insofar as handling problems individually is concerned, it also gives you tremendous flexibility. Understanding these kinds of priorities gives you room to operate effectively and sets the tone for learning.

You also need to recognize the difference between being a teacher and being a buddy to your students. Too often, being a buddy is nothing more than laziness and bribery disguised. Teaching is a performing art. However, if you think that to win respect you need to entertain your students rather than teach them, you are headed down the wrong road. The primary purpose of having children go to school is to educate them. On the first day, it's important for us to get this priority straight in our minds. You are an educator, a mentor, a counselor, and a coach. But you are not an entertainer. You want students to like you, of course. You want them to enjoy class. However, being a buddy or an

16

entertainer to your students won't make you a competent and professional educator.

There's no doubt that children like being entertained. Some students may even mistake a teacher who is a buddy for a good teacher. But don't be confused by your role. It's a mistake that can hurt students and teachers alike. The teacher is the one who has to make this distinction for students, by showing them that there can be a climate of respect and caring without introducing unhealthy components. Once again, it's your choice to make, not the decision of the students.

WHEN BAD BEHAVIOR BECOMES THE NORM, INVITATIONS TO MISBEHAVIOR HAVE BEEN SENT

Students do make choices—following your choice, of course. They can even choose to make or break a class with their behavior. It's a simple fact: If a roomful of students decides to be disruptive and sabotage a teacher's effort, it can be done. However, be aware that one important factor is often forgotten here: Some kind of "invitation" has almost always been offered by the teacher to students when bad behavior becomes the norm.

This invitation may come in the form of poor preparation, treating students in less than considerate ways, or challenging them with a power play. In truth, students' behavior is often merely a response to our behavior. If this isn't so, then why is it that the same children act properly in other classes? Never forget, children are good at picking up cues. They are also masters at translating these invitations into terms that serve them. Fortunately, misbehavior usually doesn't arise when the teacher has chosen to be the classroom learning leader, help students be successful, and share power and responsibility in the process. Therefore, always keep in mind that if students don't have any responsibility in learning in the classroom, then there is no partnership. Above all, you must recognize that with any responsibility comes a degree of power.

When you enter the classroom, you're center stage. It's your choice to be the best teacher your students will ever encounter, or to forfeit the challenge. If you are a professional in the best sense,

A Choice
Students
Don't Have

there isn't the slightest doubt about what your choice should be. And if you make that choice, you will help your students to make the same choice regarding their efforts in the classroom. Furthermore, your choice will determine whether or not you get order and control—prerequisites for successful teaching.

CHAPTER

4

ORDER, CONTROL, AND YOU

Order and control are subjects which have long dominated teacher attention. We worry and fret about both, whether we are new or experienced teachers. There's added pressure in the fact that everyone, students and colleagues alike, will know whether we can or cannot establish order in our classroom. Too, our ability or inability to establish order in our room affects other teachers. If our room is disorderly, one of our colleagues may experience difficulty when students go to their next class. And this difficulty is the result of our failure. Yet, we must not take the wrong road in our efforts to achieve order. If we do, we may destroy our relationship with students in the process. We won't, if we come early to the realization that order and control are not one and the same. There is a vast difference between the two.

ORDER CAN'T BE FORCED OR DEMANDED, REGARDLESS OF OUR DESIRES

Providing order is a teacher's responsibility—and duty. We owe it to students, for if we can't establish order, we can't teach. And if we can't teach, students can't learn. However, experience will tell us quickly that we can't legislate order, even though we might like to. We can't insist on it, force it, or demand it, and then be effective as a partner with students in the learning process.

Order is best established by being orderly ourselves. The roots of good classroom order lie in lesson preparation—and our ability

19

to relate lessons in a meaningful, interesting, and relevant way. You will never know a good teacher who doesn't have order. Likewise, you will never know a teacher who doesn't have order to be a good one—even though many want everyone to believe they are.

One thing is certain: A lack of order isn't the fault of students, whether we want to admit it or not. This truth is proven time and again when disorderly students go to another teacher and become orderly. It's also a fact that some teachers lose order at specific times, especially at the beginning or toward the end of the hour or day. More often than not, this is because they weren't prepared to teach the whole hour or day. Let us never forget this reality in our search for order and control. If we want students to be orderly, we must be orderly. Above all, we must have a reason for them to be orderly.

DOMINANCE WILL NOT GIVE THE ORDER WHICH FACILITATES LEARNING

Control of a classroom of students is a direct derivative of order. The kind of control we should seek is that which enhances order—rather than that which implies dominance. There's a wide difference.

Unfortunately, seeking to dominate or control is one of the biggest and most common mistakes teachers make. When a teacher attempts to attain control with threats, promises, fear, or force, all that is necessary for a productive teacher-student learning situation is lost in the process. If force or fear is our primary tool for gaining control, then we are working for the wrong kind of control. Too, we will always find that forced control requires that we constantly do one thing—apply more force or fear. Some teachers are continually engaged in this futile struggle, and their peace of mind and teaching effectiveness get lost in the battle. The kind of control you need as a classroom teacher comes out of order. Too often, many of the mistakes we make and the problems we encounter come out of trying first to establish order by controlling students. It won't work.

Remember, classroom control does not imply that a teacher needs total domination of a situation. When we seek to dominate, we must always operate from a center stage of power. Even class discussion requires teacher dominance. So does getting out of seats to get materials, or going to recess, the auditorium, or the cafeteria. This kind of control gets between us and students, and hinders learning as well as deflates the teacher-student-class relationship. Teachers who seek this kind of control feel helpless when they are not in total control—and worn out physically and mentally when they are. They feel vulnerable. They fear that a situation they can't handle may develop. Therefore, they feel they must be involved in everything. In the meantime, they feel stress and pressure unknown to the master teacher. They are totally regimented teachers who think learning is taking place in the classroom when, indeed, it is not.

Without doubt, if force or fear is constantly applied in the classroom, it may control students' physical actions—but it cannot and will not control their thinking. In truth, no teacher can control or dominate the minds of students. And no teacher should want to. That's exactly why we should never approach students in a way that indicates we are seeking to dominate them.

Our job is to help students control their own lives—not to control their lives for them. This is the only way they can become self-disciplined. Of vital importance, we must realize that when order is established, the control which is necessary to facilitate learning will follow.

MAKE NO MISTAKE: CLASSROOM CONTROL DOESN'T MEAN LEARNING IS TAKING PLACE

The presence of control in a classroom doesn't necessarily mean learning is taking place. Therefore, your responsibility lies in setting the tone and climate from which order can result. The structure you choose in order to generate learning in the classroom has a much better chance of being readily accepted if you join with those you lead—rather than structure a separation through the use of control techniques.

The first day of school is a time when you should begin developing ties with students—not creating gaps. You begin by making yourself a learning partner with students. Your initial efforts to establish order begin with your own attitude toward order—for yourself and others. This attitude is reflected in what you say and how you say it. Most of all, it is reflected in the order you reveal in yourself. In truth, when a teacher is not prepared to deal with academics and people, there is no reason for students to be orderly.

Your biggest teaching advantage will come when students realize that there are simply too many things of importance happening in the classroom for them to be preoccupied with being disorderly. This is your primary key in establishing a climate for order. If you are going to have a successful school year, you must have order. You must also have control. But you won't get either if you look upon them as one and the same. Let's look at the real powers you need in the classroom. These are the powers which enhance your probability for success.

CHAPTER

5

THE REAL
POWERS
YOU NEED

Teachers have always held firm opinions regarding what is needed to get classes off to a good start. We have assumed that one of these needs is authority or power. In fact, we may make some quick first day judgments regarding how easy or difficult it will be to establish our authority in the classroom. The first judgment we truly need to make, however, has nothing to do with the powers we must hold over students. Rather, it has to do with the powers we will need in order to control ourselves if we are going to achieve any measure of excellence in teaching this year. There are three powers we must exercise: starting power, staying power, and finishing power. All three must stem from a professional attitude and careful planning of the time, events, and situations that occur in a school.

IT TAKES AN OPEN ACT OF DETERMINATION TO BEGIN THE YEAR SIGNIFICANTLY

The first teacher power you need is starting power. And starting power has nothing to do with rules and regulations. You need thorough lesson plans designed to give all children a measure of success in the classroom. Lesson plans that guarantee the failure of some students also guarantee that those students will not participate in class. You need exciting and flexible plans that you intend to initiate immediately—not next week or next month.

It takes an open act of determination to start something

significant in the classroom. As a teacher, you are the only one in the classroom with the power to begin with a plan designed to help every child be successful. If you don't begin teaching immediately in such a significant way, you and your students may be behind more quickly than you can imagine. That's because you are teaching more than a grade or a course. You're teaching people. And remember, your primary task is to pick up students where they are academically when they begin your class, and take them as far as they can go. Sometimes teachers don't. In fact, their whole attitude may shift into negative when they see that their students aren't ready academically to begin their classes or courses. This is the point at which many teachers begin failing on the very first day of school. They aren't prepared with the power to start because they have made no allowance for the fact that students enter the classroom with different learning achievements, abilities, and skills.

When school begins, many teachers evaluate where students are academically—and then throw in the towel on some students. Some teachers may even say to their students: "You're not even prepared for this class" or "What did you do last year?" Such an action is both a mistake and a professional misjudgment. After all, a teacher's starting point is the starting point of students, not the starting point of a textbook or a lesson plan. This year—and in all the years to come—all students in your classes will never begin out of the same starting gate. Understand this reality—and don't fight it or you will never achieve the professional attitude or skills you need to start the year successfully. And you must have the power to start reaching all students the day they walk into your classroom.

TO HAVE A GOOD YEAR,
WE ALL NEED STAYING POWER

If a successful year is to lie ahead, you'll also need staying power. It's one thing to make the move that gets things on the road. It's quite another to keep them going. In truth, the initial thrust in teaching is often a mechanical move. However, step two requires artistry. It requires that you support what is being learned by offering additional information and encouraging students to continue the search themselves.

You can keep students' momentum going and enthusiasm high

only if your own match or exceed theirs. Nothing is more dampening to students than to find that adult leadership lacks interest or is dying a quick death. Staying power is necessary for continuous learning, and you are the only one with the power to make learning continue to happen. Don't be the kind of teacher who is "all talk and no show." Such teachers talk big on the first day of school. By Thanksgiving, however, they act as if they are bored to death with teaching—and then wonder why students are losing interest.

You need staying power because teaching is just plain hard work. At least, it is for good teachers. It's no easy task to face a roomful of students with different aptitudes and backgrounds, and help them learn to the best of their abilities. Students learn at different rates. Some may hardly learn at all. If you cannot accept such a reality, you should not be a teacher. Without staying power, you're likely to give up and quit on some students. And giving up is a privilege you do not have as a professional educator.

THE FINISHING TOUCH INCLUDES ORGANIZING VARIED AND UNRELATED MATERIALS INTO MEANINGFUL AND RELEVANT FORMS

The final power you need this year is finishing power. You'll need it in terms of both individual lessons and the entire year. Sometimes, teachers think that finishing just happens. It doesn't, especially in learning. Finishing power is the ability to organize varied and apparently unrelated material into a form that makes it meaningful and relevant. This teacher touch is the bow on the package. Without it the effect of learning is more disorganized than organized. You need to remember to tie the bow on each lesson, on every unit, and on the whole year.

This school year will last approximately thirty-six weeks. You should be directing your effort toward helping students achieve their only realistic and reasonable goal—improvement. This means student achievement should reflect continuous growth throughout the year.

Most of the powers you will need this year have nothing to do with students. They have to do with you. That's why you need not worry about putting students in the kind of situation which enables you to be the authority over them. Your task is to use the strengths of a teacher's starting, staying, and finishing powers as tools for successful teaching.

How well you teach this year has to do with both your abilities and your attitudes. If you can't get and stay enthusiastic about what you are teaching, it's very unlikely that students will do so. Then, a good finish is improbable. If you see only a classroom full of students rather than individuals, it's not likely that you will relate to those you are trying to teach. You must see students and their differences as challenging possibilities rather than only as problems. When you do, you will see the possibilities in yourself as well. It's the challenge that students present that will give you the enthusiasm, excitement, and stamina to generate the real powers you need for every lesson, all year long. Therefore, we can go no further without talking about the need for a teacher to be positive. It is a topic we all talk about and readily accept, but one that few of us really practice continually because we don't fully understand its significance.

CHAPTER

6

BE
POSITIVE

For successful people, a positive approach to life is as essential as breathing. But unlike the involuntary act of breathing, being positive is a trained behavioral pattern that must be practiced daily to be perfected. Being positive is not easy. If it were, everyone would be a positive person. Moreover, being positive is more than an attitude toward living: It's a way of life.

Remember, teaching is sharing. Teaching is adjusting. Teaching is adapting to the needs of others. This aspect of teaching makes it unique among the professions. As expert as he or she is, the doctor doesn't really adjust—the patient does. Law doesn't apply to the individual case, and neither does the lawyer—the client adapts to the law. Only in education does the professional, if he or she is effective and successful, adapt, adjust, and share himself or herself with each individual person being taught. This is one of the primary reasons teachers must maintain and develop a positive attitude if they expect to find rewards both for those they intend to teach and for themselves.

UNFORTUNATELY, ADOPTING A NEGATIVE VIEWPOINT IS EXTREMELY EASY

It's easy for teachers to become negative. We can thoroughly believe that one child is completely destroying our teaching plan. In fact, one word of negative support from another teacher can convince us that some or all children are "bad." Unfortunately, compliments from students and parents can be few and far

27

between. These and many other factors can distort a teacher's thinking and blind him or her to the real truth.

To achieve a positive approach to teaching, you must strengthen your relationships with positive and successful people. You simply can't associate with negative people—or those who are unhappy in education—and remain positive. The human environment is important to your development. Therefore, give yourself the benefit of associating primarily with the positive people in your profession without allowing yourself to judge those who are not.

Likewise, keep your perspective regarding the normalities of school. For instance, every school has student discipline problems. The vast majority of students are living up to their school responsibilities and preparing for a better life. More times than I care to remember, however, a teacher has come close to personal and professional ruin because of one or two discipline problems. Likewise, teachers can easily become negative about such things as intercom announcements, assemblies, athletic events and other extra-class activities, and even noise in the halls, because of the actions of a handful of students. We can become negative because of interruptions, schedule changes, and class size.

When you find yourself beginning to think negatively, think instead about surviving. Every time you begin to become negative, realize that you are beginning to die professionally. Refuse to waste your talent or energy trying to search out or accept difficulty. Instead, hunt for constructive possibilities. Remember, negative people are the stones that other people walk on when they climb to success. Know that negative teachers are those who are continually reminding themselves of what they can't do, won't do, and fear to try. Your basic need for survival should help you avoid sowing the seeds of your own failure through negative thoughts and actions.

MAKE NO MISTAKE: OPERATING OUT OF NEGATIVES MAKES EVERYTHING DIFFICULT

Being negative is of double significance in the lives of teachers. If you are negative with colleagues, you are probably negative with students as well. It's almost impossible to be otherwise, for negativism is a personality trait that soon becomes a dominant way of life.

Certainly, we should never turn our heads against truth. However, we can't automatically respond, "I can't" or "No way" to everything facing us. Negative people are not objective. They turn off to everything—sometimes without even knowing what they are doing. The fact remains that negativism is contrary to the entire educational process.

Don't be misled. Operating from a negative position makes life difficult, because negativism is so demoralizing and self-defeating. Once we have learned how to be positive, it is much easier to function from this stance. As teachers, we must remember that for every negative we offer, we give nothing. But with every positive we propose, we have, in truth, suggested a course of action. This is the basis for the practicality of the positive. Positive people, people who are doers, who live life to its fullest, simply cannot function from any other platform.

The motivation, stimulation, and confidence needed to begin anything with a probability for success are impaired by negativism. You need to be positive—if for no other reason than to avoid being consumed by the certain failure inherent in being negative. The teacher who neither understands nor cares about the tremendous force of positives and negatives in his or her own life, as well as in the lives of students, will never find success or happiness in teaching.

The need for positives is a *practical part* of everyday existence. Without positives, hopelessness replaces hope. Likewise, you must be the first to recognize that people *always* relate more easily to optimism than to pessimism. Students are not the exception. Students learn much more readily when teachers emphasize the positive rather than the other side of the coin. Remember, the complications that result from dwelling on the negative can make mountains out of molehills. Therefore, watch yourself closely. Make sure you aren't issuing more *don'ts* than *do's* and more *can'ts* than *can's* in your teaching. This teaching approach is more than the beginning of negative thinking—it is negative action.

We know that being positive is a state of mind. It is a mental outlook. It is attained by looking for the possible rather than the impossible. It is holding hope rather than embracing hopelessness.

You can begin by revealing that you don't have to understand people to accept them. The next step is avoiding automatic rejection—and not always reading between the lines in what people do or say. Whenever your criticisms are not accompanied by objective thought, you must always back up. After automatically saying, "I don't think we can do it," you must add, "But on second thought, let's take a look and see if we can." In addition, be fully aware of the significance of positives for students. By its very nature, being positive gives students a sense of well-being in your presence. Realize that a student has a positive or negative experience every time he or she looks into the face of a teacher. As simple as it seems, eye contact, approving nods, winks, and smiles show students they are worth smiling at—and the first positive step has been taken. Acceptance is always the first step toward being positive. All else follows this human connection.

All along the way, small teacher actions can mean the difference between encouragement and discouragement for a student. If a teacher *sighs* often and treats the whole process of teaching as a wearisome nonevent, students can't help feeling and accepting a sense of responsibility for this teacher attitude. Unfortunately, students can't know that a negative teacher attitude has little or nothing to do with them. That's a terrible negative imposition. Yet, it is the frightful truth about negatives. When we offer a negative, we offer more harm than it might seem. In truth, by this imposition, we add an extra burden which someone else must overcome. That's why, in our lives as teachers, we have a practical need for positives, for students as well as for ourselves.

Without a positive attitude toward yourself, students, parents, colleagues, administrators, and the work of the school, it's highly unlikely that you will be very successful in teaching. To attain this level of functioning, you must be flexible. Let's discuss this need because it is so vitally important to a teacher's success and well-being. After all, it is neither a common nor a natural characteristic of many educators.

CHAPTER
7

BE
FLEXIBLE

It would be wonderful if teachers truly liked all the diversity that occurs daily in a school. But many do not. They like the security of routine. Change causes a need for adjustments by teachers, students, and staff. Therefore, change is often a threat to a teacher's basic need for security.

Interruptions are a challenge to a teacher's ability. They force adjustments that teachers honestly don't know if they can make. Sometimes, they ruin teacher planning. Teachers often feel that interruptions prevent them from doing the job they know they can do. Interruptions and change interfere with subject-matter instruction. They give teachers the feeling that others believe everything else is more important than what they are doing in the classroom. Interruptions give teachers the feeling that athletics, assemblies, announcements, and counselor visits all have priority over classroom instruction. When teachers have these feelings, they get upset. Sometimes they want to explode!

Yet, in reality, we know these feelings are not justified. All school time is class time, because learning occurs throughout the entire school day. Teachers must realize, therefore, that the vast majority of interruptions which occur during the day must occur during class time. Accommodating to change, disturbance, and interruption—difficult as that may be—is a part of teaching. Similarly, medicine would probably be an easier profession if people did not get sick or have babies at night. But we trust the physician to perform as well emotionally and professionally at 3 a.m. as he or she does at 3 p.m. For all professionals, flexibility is mandatory.

FLEXIBILITY MUST BE LEARNED BECAUSE IF YOU'RE NOT FLEXIBLE, YOU CAN'T TEACH

The ability to be flexible is learned. Teachers must train themselves thoroughly in the art of flexibility, or they will encounter problems on a daily basis that will impair their efficiency and effectiveness in the classroom, as well as their mental health.

If all teachers could sit in the principal's office for one week, they would be amazed at the turmoil caused by an early dismissal for a ball game, a child held out of class by another teacher, an unscheduled assembly, a bulletin not delivered to the classroom, or even an unexpected intercom announcement. Administrators are aware of the chaos that can result from interruptions.

Yet, many teachers blame administrators for all these interruptions. True, administrators should hold classroom interruptions to a minimum. But if teachers expect interruptions to be a rare occurrence in any school under normal conditions, they are being unrealistic. This is a fact of teaching and school scheduling.

Becoming frustrated because of these situations is not abnormal. But reacting overtly in an unprofessional way, losing composure, or making an issue and involving other teachers is not a sign of maturity. Certainly, failing to become more flexible with experience is abnormal.

Flexibility is, in the final analysis, a state of mind that must be learned. If you aren't flexible, you can't teach. If you're unable emotionally to accept constant change, you're in the wrong profession.

Remember, the more complex the task and the more people involved in that task, the greater the need for individual flexibility. The very nature of education makes teacher flexibility a necessity. That's why you must continue to function effectively regardless of interruption or change. Teaching yourself the art of acting and reacting as the ever-changing school situation demands is what will make you a master teacher.

CHAPTER
8

IF
YOU WANT
RESPECT

Respect is a primary factor in determining a teacher's success or failure. The best way to get respect from students is to give it. However, respect comes in different packages. It isn't a single *something* to be granted, lectured on, or demanded. There are many kinds of respect in a school, and if you want to be respected you must be aware of them all.

For instance, there is respect for knowledge. We all know the teacher who is respected for his or her knowledge. A teacher must be a scholar—because we can't generate scholars without being scholars ourselves. Most certainly, without a scholarly approach to teaching, we can't expect to be respected as teachers. But there are other forms of respect.

Consider respect for time. Some teachers feel that it's a great injustice if a faculty meeting adjourns late. Yet, they think nothing of giving the entire class a two-hour assignment as punishment for the misbehavior of one or two students. Such teacher action is likely to bring disrespect rather than respect.

Also, think of respect in terms of privacy. Most teachers would be outraged if their shortcomings were discussed with anyone. Yet, some teachers will discuss the faults of their students with anyone who will listen. In the lounge or at any gathering, they are apt to criticize students by name. No action could possibly be more disrespectful of student privacy.

Respect is also revealed in courtesy. When we do something for a student, custodian, or secretary, we expect to be thanked. Yet, we may make demands of these people daily and take their services for granted without ever thinking of saying, "Thank you." Courtesy is a two-way street—and a catalyst for respect. So is regard for the work and feelings of others.

One thing is certain: Those teachers who show respect in the way they treat people and handle the responsibilities of their teaching are the most apt to be liked as well as respected. You must work hard to earn respect—and to keep it. If you lose the respect of others, the cause is more likely something you've done than something they've done. It's this understanding that can keep you from moving in the wrong direction to get respect.

THERE IS A CORRELATION
BETWEEN RESPECT AND SUCCESS

There is a direct relationship between the degree of respect you earn and the degree of effectiveness you achieve as a professional teacher. Respect cannot be demanded, forced, or compromised—and once lost it is difficult to regain. Your self-esteem is dependent upon the respect you receive just as the self-esteem of others is dependent on the respect you extend to them. That's the mutuality inherent in respect.

A person who is respected is usually respected by everyone. You'll seldom find a teacher who is respected by students but not by colleagues. But you will want more than respect as a teacher. You will want to be liked too. That's why you must treat students as you want and need to be treated yourself.

We need to be liked by our students, whether we want to admit it or not. They need us to like them too. That's why being liked and respected are vital elements in our relationships with each other. Nothing of importance will happen for us or our students without a degree of mutual liking and respect. Remembering these facts can prevent us from making various mistakes with our interpersonal relationships in a school. If you want to be successful, you'll devote as much effort to showing respect for others as you devote to seeking respect from them.

CHAPTER
9

AN
EIGHT-STEP
PLAN
FOR THE
FIRST DAY

Often, students walk into our classrooms on the first day of school with some positive and negative conclusions about us. This is one reason that we need to have a solid plan for the first day. Whether we're on a shortened or a full-day schedule, we might consider doing at least eight things during our first contact with students. That is, we might if we intend to get off to a good start.

NEGATIVE RULES, REGULATIONS, REQUIREMENTS, AND DEMANDS WON'T DRAW STUDENTS TO YOU

First, we should openly, freely, and emphatically promise students the biggest benefit of our class or course. It should be the biggest advantage students can expect to gain during the year. And we should tell students that we intend to work hard to deliver this benefit to them.

Second, we need to elaborate upon this benefit in clear and specific ways. In the process, we should bring forth all the other benefits—and be positive, enthusiastic, and inclusive as we do. Remember, different benefits will draw different students to us and our teaching. Negative rules, regulations, requirements, and demands won't. Too often, we talk to students the very first minute about what they *can't* do or what they *have* to do—rather than what they *get* to do. We can relate, both in general and in specific ways, what they can expect to learn which will be of benefit to them personally. Do not believe, even for a moment, that these benefits are "understood" or "obvious," or that students see how they will benefit from learning in your classroom. They do not.

Third, we should back all the statements we make with facts or proof so that students will find what we say believable. If we can, we should relate stories of former students—without giving names—and use state and national statistics which back our claims.

WE SHOULD FINISH THE FIRST DAY BY
TEACHING A LESSON ALL STUDENTS CAN USE

Fourth, we need to reveal the specific ways students will lose if they don't take full advantage of our class or course. In the process, we should try not to arouse any fears. We won't if we simply state these realities or beliefs in a factual way. Remember, if we instill fear as we give our first day message, our words will lose their value as a motivating force. Fifth, at this point, we ought to sum up what we have said. As we do, we should rephrase all the major benefits revealed. This action is necessary for positive reinforcement. We need to ask students—individually and as a group—to work, study, and learn during the year. If we fail to ask students individually for such a commitment, many will believe that what we said applies to classmates—but not to them. Seventh, we need to remind students that they are beginning the new school year with a clean slate, and that past incidents have no bearing on the upcoming year. Eighth, we should end the class with a vital objective: teaching a lesson. Our objective should be to have *all* students leave the first day having learned something that they can use immediately. This step cannot be left out of our first-day plan.

In delivering this eight-step plan, we should take care to avoid certain pitfalls. For instance, we must be careful about qualifying our first-day message. We shouldn't indicate that some students will do well and that some won't. Nor should we indicate that we're certain some will take full advantage while others will not—or that we have high expectations for some and no expectations for others. Remember, our expectations as well as our enthusiasm to teach all students must come through loud and clear.

It's also a mistake to try to make sure students know who is the boss. Your position tells students you're the teacher in the classroom. How you function will tell them whether you're up to the task. Therefore, avoid the pitfall of telling all students—when you're really only trying to reach one or two—that you're tough and mean business, and that they shouldn't try to fool you or buck you. Some teachers try to come off as "hard-nosed" on the first day—then they're surprised when students don't want any part of them or what they are teaching. The advice, "Don't smile till Christmas" or "Start tough—you can always let up" is not good advice. Such a stance only forms bad first impressions. And it's insulting to the vast majority of students who do not deserve to be treated in such a way.

REMEMBER, IT IS THE POSITIVES THAT WILL GIVE US AND STUDENTS THE BEST CHANCE FOR A GOOD YEAR

The first day of school is one of the most important days of the year. Students see us for the first time. They size us up as competent or incompetent, nice or mean, fair or unfair, and caring or uncaring. And the opinions they form, good or bad, can be influenced by our actions and can get in the way of our teaching and students' learning.

That's why we need to begin with a positive. This is not the time or place for the negative. And we ought not switch from being positive to being negative because of one student—or our own fears. Rather, we need to stick to the constructive motivation of the positive. This is most easily achieved by giving students benefits for being in our classes. After all, the benefits we provide will help students "buy into" what we have planned for them this year. And by proclaiming the benefits, we have the best chance for a good start and a good year—and so do students.

CHAPTER
10

DON'T
TAKE YOUR PROBLEMS
TO SCHOOL

There are some rules for human behavior, standards of professional conduct, and common-sense human actions of which we are very much aware if we intend to be successful. Yet, as human beings, we often find it extremely difficult to practice them continually and habitually. One such rule is this: Don't take your personal problems to school. Above all, never impose them upon students!

VIOLATING THE RULES OF PROFESSIONAL CONDUCT HAS CONSEQUENCES

Every teacher is aware of this standard for professional conduct. We are even aware of the consequences of violating it. We realize, for instance, that when a problem in our personal lives is expressed at school, our personal problems can spread like a cancer into our professional lives. We know that our dispositions can cause us to hurt children and colleagues alike by attitude, word, and action. We realize that we sometimes "bite students' heads off" the minute they open their mouths. We may react negatively to every suggestion from a colleague, or became catty, sarcastic, or picky. We can demand the attention of our friends exclusively to listen to, and attempt to understand, our problems. We know we shouldn't. We don't want to be this way—but what can we do when these periods of trouble enter our lives?

First, we must realize that, because of our humanness, we tend to believe that any problem is big. Most certainly, many problems people face are big. Medical problems, those involving family emotional crises, and financial problems often require professional help. Therefore, we should seek help outside the school and never on school time. However, relatively speaking, most of our problems are small. Regardless of the size of our problems, we deal with them in one of two ways: Either we solve them, or we try to cope with them and learn to live with them, though often unsatisfactorily. The real danger, of course, is that if we don't solve our problems, they may build to the point that we cannot live with any degree of happiness or operate with any degree of effectiveness until they are eliminated.

GUIDELINES FOR KEEPING YOUR APPROACH PROFESSIONAL RATHER THAN PERSONAL

Here are some things you can do to prevent taking your problems to school.

First, recognize the foul mood you are in. If you don't, you can't possibly compensate for your troubled state of mind. Tell yourself before you walk through the doors in the morning that your mood is not the best and that, therefore, you will compensate for it today.

When you arrive at school, make it a point to see the happy and positive people on the staff. At all costs avoid those who you can predict will be in the same mood you are in. Remind yourself that, because you're not at your mental best today, you will try to avoid any offending encounters with others. People who don't have these conversations with themselves not only miss a sure way to professional growth, but also overlook their best problem solver—themselves.

Though you may find it difficult to believe, the vast majority of people who take their troubles to work can directly relate their mood to the time they get up in the morning. Mornings can be a bad time. This is especially true for the teacher with children of his or her own. Perhaps a wife can't get her husband awake, or the kids off to school or to the babysitter on time—and no one eats an adequate breakfast. She yells at everybody—then goes to school to take care of someone else's children with the guilty feeling that she's not caring for her own. The same is true for the man who feels he is a good teacher but a poor father and husband because of the things that happen in the morning at home—all because of twenty or thirty minutes' extra sleep. These teachers don't even have time in the morning to right their wrongs before leaving for work. They feel too heavily the pressure of time, and it results in inhuman treatment toward those they love the most.

Too, some teachers may find that the only time they have to themselves is that time before the family arises. They need those quiet moments. They're faced with bedlam in the morning, school all day, and family responsibilities in the evening. You may find that rising thirty minutes earlier in the morning can literally change your entire outlook. It is, at least, worth your consideration.

Music helps too. Pleasant music in the morning is a tranquilizer when things aren't going right. If you drive to work alone, turn on the radio and don't be ashamed to sing along as you drive to school. Sound silly? You would be surprised to know how many people use the medicine of music every day—regardless of their mood.

Though it is difficult at the time, try putting your problems in true perspective. Sometimes you can laugh at them. Don't forget that if they are indeed laughable, you should allow your family to laugh at them with you. Tension can ease when family members realize you don't consider your problems as serious as they thought you did. Remember, when you leave home *uptight* it may ruin another person's day too.

KEEP IN MIND THAT STUDENTS HAVE PERSONAL PROBLEMS TOO

You must be continually aware that everyone has personal problems, and often they all seem big. You must know that even though you can expect to have them, you cannot be totally prepared for their arrival. The jolt of their arrival can produce many normal human reactions such as crying, yelling, anger, guilt, and withdrawal. Normally, these initial emotions are followed by an attempt to solve the problem. Yet, some people never try to solve their problems—because they never get beyond the emotion stage.

There is one self-reminder that can always help you to regain professional perspective, one that prevents you from taking your

41

problems to school: Remember your students. Be aware that, because of circumstances at home and elsewhere, students may be forced to bring problems to school that are much greater than yours. And they may not be in a position to solve these problems—often they can only live with them. Therefore, never do anything that would cause your students to come to school and find another problem like the one at home, or a worse problem, because of you. When a child has a problem at home, at least he or she has some opportunity to escape temporarily. The child can go to his or her room, to the yard or the streets, or to visit a friend. At school, students can only sit at their desks and "take it." If you remember these realities, you may be better positioned to leave your problems at the door.

CHAPTER
11

DO YOU
REALLY BELIEVE
IN LEARNING?

Certainly, whether or not we believe in learning is a very important question—and it needs to be followed by other questions before we offer a reply. For instance, do we really think that what we are doing in schools and in the classroom is significant? Do we honestly believe that what we are teaching makes a difference in the lives of students?

If you say that you as an educator believe in learning, how do you feel about what's happening in classrooms other than yours? Do your attitudes and behavior reflect to students and colleagues alike that you cherish learning? If you asked your students whether they believe you cherish learning, would they answer, "Yes, you do," "No, you don't," or "Sometimes you do, and sometimes you don't"?

How you demonstrate your belief in learning is vitally important. You must make sure your students know, from your words and actions, that you do, indeed, cherish learning. If they don't believe you do, then they probably won't either.

LEARNING IS TAKING PLACE EVERYWHERE
CHILDREN WORK AND PLAY

Learning is an amalgam of many elements. Your acceptance of this fact is important to your professional perspective. So is your awareness of the fact that meaningful learning is taking place in gyms, labs, halls, playgrounds, and classrooms other than yours.

More important, you need to realize that some kind of learning is taking place for every child, every minute of his or her waking hours.

If you believe in learning, you will always promote learning to students. And you will never quit trying to make learning happen for them. You will know that not all learning comes from the formal curriculum. In truth, the motivation for learning comes more from teacher attitude and approach than it does from the textbooks students use. That's why you need to understand what students experience as they learn.

When students are gaining knowledge, they are searching. So are we as teachers. Often, although the learning goal has been established, the method of arriving at it has not. Both we and our students are traveling uncharted terrain—with an excitement all its own. Sometimes, the surprise we both experience in the process of discovering how to learn will convert a small spark of enthusiasm into a brilliant flame, and we take off in directions we hadn't even thought possible. That excitement is what learning is all about—and it happens when teachers truly cherish learning. That's why you need to adopt and express positive learning attitudes if you want children to cherish learning.

YOUR ACTIONS EXPRESS YOUR ATTITUDES TOWARD LEARNING

As a teacher, there are many things you can do to show children that you cherish learning—and to help them do the same. Above all, you must show an awareness of life. You should notice everything, and demonstrate your curiosity openly. You should appreciate everything and show that, to you, all things are meaningful. Everything from asking students if they noticed the sunset last night to telling them about a new book in the library lets them see you growing. That's real learning. You can talk about books you've read. You can suggest interests students might explore. You can study along with children in class. They can see you using the media center continually. And you can always be positive when teaching. Certainly, you can't say things like "I know this is boring, but we have to cover the material," and expect students to think you enjoy and cherish learning. And when you're teaching, you can continually share your belief that learning is a two-way street. You can let students know that, as you teach them, you are learning from them—and that you enjoy it.

YOU MUST DEMONSTRATE APPRECIATION FOR ALL LEARNING AND THE WHOLE CURRICULUM

If you cherish learning, you can demonstrate appreciation for all aspects of the curriculum, including the extra-class activities curriculum. You can make sure students don't think your learning interests are limited to your grade or academic discipline. You can be visible at school functions and community activities. And, certainly, you can take the time to talk to students about their plans and interests, whatever they may be, and offer support, ideas, and suggestions that relate to those plans. Even when students talk about a vacation, you can suggest things they might want to see, or books they can read that pertain to their trips. If you really believe in learning, you will see it as a mystery and a miracle, one that is bigger than you are and broader than your classroom. And you will make sure students know your stand.

When we find out that learning itself is a mystery, we discover its meaning. Its enchantment is in allowing free flow. Its delight is in embarking on the journey and pursuing the goal. The ultimate in learning is to appreciate the meaning of the experience while we are having the experience—and trying to get in the vicinity of excellence. Flowery words? You bet. But this is the excitement and the real satisfaction in being an educator.

When you take such a course, you have grasped what learning is all about. You'll find that you don't have to declare to anyone that you believe in learning. All you need to do is embrace it. Others will see how you feel without your even having to tell them.

CHAPTER
12

SELL
YOUR WHOLE SYSTEM—
IT'S YOU

Whether you like it or not, you are continually *selling education* in your community. You must be aware of this fact. It is becoming increasingly important for every member of the school system team to become an ambassador for the whole system.

You might immediately ask, "Why is it my responsibility to sell the whole system?" Such questioning of the paramount importance of—and our responsibility for—"selling the system" is one of the primary reasons that educators are failing to instill a positive public attitude toward education.

OUR REPUTATION AFFECTS EVERYTHING,
INCLUDING US

It is every teacher's responsibility to create and maintain public confidence in his or her school system. If you don't care about how people regard education, you are a liability to the profession. Furthermore, your reputation as a professional teacher—and your effectiveness in the classroom—will suffer. If public opinion of teachers and schools is low in your community, teacher self-esteem will be low too. On the other hand, selling education gives you security. In truth, the only real security that any educator has is derived from meeting the educational needs of all the children in the community. If these needs are not being filled, the community sees less need for teachers.

When teachers begin selling their whole system, rather than just themselves, they gain the correct concept of education and of their true worth as professional teachers. They also become a tremendous asset to both the school and the system. However, *selling* and *teacher personality* sometimes conflict.

ACHIEVING BOTH NEEDS: OURS AND THE SCHOOL'S

Often it is difficult for a teacher to fulfill a need to be recognized, accepted, and appreciated as a whole, unique, and professional teacher, and at the same time to identify himself or herself as a part of a school's or system's education team. Many teachers view their individual work as all they need be concerned with.

Some teachers express a belief that there is a conflict between maintaining one's individual identity and being a part of a whole. They are wrong. The need to find individual identity—plus identity within a whole—is causing many individuals to raise questions about themselves. It may cause personal as well as professional problems. Maybe this is one of the reasons that so many people searching for individual identity simply as men and women are having so much difficulty being part of a family as fathers and husbands or wives and mothers. Frequently, being part of a whole is more difficult than being an independent individual. The need to *be ourselves* and the need to *be part of something* are within us all. Achieving success with only one, whichever one it is, makes that success less meaningful.

According to teachers, a feeling of being part of a system is the more difficult of the two identities to attain. However, there are many things you can begin doing today to become a *real part* of your whole school system.

KNOWING WHAT IS REALLY INVOLVED IN MAKING A SCHOOL FUNCTION

The classroom teacher has the "glory job" in education. Teachers are the team members who are always center stage, catching the spotlight. And many teachers can't make the *I* become *we* because they are totally unaware of what it really takes to operate a school system. They forget about the wide range of specialties and talents needed just to open the doors of the school daily. They forget, or even dismiss as unimportant, the contributions of the custodian, groundskeeper, bus driver, cook, bookkeeper, secretary, librarian, receiving room clerk, and delivery person. They forget that schools need dietitians, curriculum directors, and nurses, in addition to administrators. There's a lot more to education than teaching.

Then too, there is the contribution of the different grade levels within a system. Teachers must recognize the importance of every part of the educational structure, K-12 and beyond, if they expect to be able to sell their whole system. I have been amazed at how little elementary teachers know about junior high or middle schools and vice versa. At times, I have been extremely concerned about the contempt that some high school teachers demonstrate toward students in, and sometimes even teachers of, grades below theirs. There isn't anything worse for a system than teachers talking as if students who haven't yet reached *their* school or *their* course were academically inadequate. These feelings can totally eliminate a teacher's chance for recognizing the importance of the whole. These are the attitudes that can demoralize and destroy school systems.

DEVELOPING THE ABILITY TO TALK ABOUT EDUCATION

You can't sell education if you talk only about what you are doing in your own classroom. You really sell education when you talk about the efforts and contributions of the other teachers, departments, and schools within your system. You sell education when you talk to people about the facet of education in which they express interest. If a person asks about vocational education or business education or elementary programs, talk about that subject—or get the answers. Don't try to switch every educational inquiry to your subject area.

Realistically, teachers have difficulty selling their systems because, too many times, they are interested only in their own academic areas, and don't know anything about any other discipline or level. You must change the *I* to *we* to gain knowledge about your system.

Some teachers visualize themselves as the whole, and cannot see themselves as a part of anything. Many people go through life refusing to be a part of anything—family, church, community, or even country—without ever realizing that it's through being part of these things that a person attains fulfillment. Sometimes we forget that parts make a whole, and wholes are made of parts. With one small part missing, there is no longer a whole. This is as true for the school system team as it is for any other group.

Every time you talk to someone about education, *a sale is made*. Every single contact results in your selling people on the job the schools are doing—or in people selling you on the fact that they don't believe the schools are doing their job. Remember, people aren't buying you as an individual teacher; they are buying the whole educational system. Never forget, the public is intelligent enough to understand that people generally don't buy the salesman—they buy the company. But, as far as most are concerned, the salesman *is* the company. People are smart enough to know that you, as a teacher, are only as good as your system is—so be as smart as they are.

If you can't think of yourself as a salesman, then call yourself an ambassador. Then, represent your whole system—it's you.

CHAPTER
13

WE'RE ALL
ON THE
SAME TEAM

Nearly all of your work as a teacher involves individual effort. You teach alone. You face problems alone. You are confined to the classroom for most of the day, isolated from other adults. You might not even know what is going on down the hall from your classroom, much less in other schools in your district. These realities do not alter the fact that, whatever you do in education, you are part of the total educational picture. Neither do they change the fact that if you truly intend to be a complete educator, you need to know what is happening to students throughout the entire educational process.

A PROFESSIONAL STANCE: DIFFERENT
FUNCTIONS, SAME MISSION

As professional educators we must do all we can to solidify education rather than divide it. We must adopt a professional stance of togetherness. Seeing ourselves and our colleagues as parts of a whole is a necessity if we are to maximize opportunities for students. Whether we teach first, seventh, or twelfth grade, we are all part of the same effort. Our attitudes toward one another will be reflected in the education received by those we teach. Make no mistake about this reality. Whether we are custodians or teachers, we are all on the same team. We all have the same mission. It is only our functions in fulfilling our mission which differ.

Remember, no teaching assignment is more important or more significant than another. Likewise, you must recognize that no segment of a school or system can falter without a ripple effect being set up within the entire school system. The total school and system can run smoothly only through joint effort. Unless every single member of the school staff understands and works according to this principle, it does not take long to disrupt the state of education in our schools.

In truth, failure to practice a general acceptance of one another is one of the reasons we're experiencing many problems in education today. Part of the reason we may not accept one another is that we don't know enough about one another. Elementary and secondary people don't know enough about each other. Many teachers don't know enough about the curriculum of grade levels other than their own. Unfortunately, every time we downgrade someone or fail to see the contribution of a colleague, we feel a little less significant ourselves. That's because we are all—in every way—on the same team and part of the same process.

THERE CANNOT BE A TEAM EFFORT WITHOUT A TEAM SPIRIT

The team effort in the total education picture is everything—but there cannot be an effective team effort unless there is team spirit as well. That's why you need to know what *professional* team spirit is, and how it differs from other kinds. For instance, athletic team spirit calls for a lot of yelling and clapping. Cheering seems to be the main ingredient in the athletic mix, and the spirit can be turned off and on by cheerleaders or turned on by a score by "our team." It is a sort of mechanical revving up that is marked by a crescendo of enthusiasm. Such an expression of team spirit is appropriate and acceptable under athletic circumstances. But no one really expects the spirit to last much past the game itself. It's an easily elicited surface expression, and not really a very serious thing once the moment is over.

For teachers, professional team spirit is much less definable and tangible. But it is extremely important. Perhaps it's the most important factor if we really want our schools to function, not on a plateau of mediocrity, but at the heights of elegance and excellence that result from contagious enthusiasm.

You should realize that professional team spirit stems from being happy in education. First and foremost, team spirit is simply joy in being a teacher and in being part of a particular school and system. This means that we can and do accept each other as professional educators. We can't have team spirit and be isolationists. "Team" means "group." To gain a sense of unity, we must function from a platform of broad involvement with all school people and all school programs. Things can't be put in compartments. We must be professionally safe with each other. No one is out to "get" anyone else, nor is anyone trying to sabotage the work of another educator. We realize that a complete, comprehensive education is impossible for a child unless the entire staff team is valued openly. Without team spirit, you will never feel you are part of the whole. Instead, you will simply feel isolated.

A STANCE OF MUTUAL TRUST WILL ENHANCE OUR ATTITUDES AND ACTIONS

The chain reaction of shared participation in education is enormous. When teachers accept one another and don't feel they have special territory to protect, team spirit thrives. It's when educators share in positive ways that we get the work of education done— totally and in healthy ways. The beneficiaries are students and staff alike.

We manage to come to such a point through mutual trust. When we infuse mutual trust with the intangibles of accepting, supporting, and giving, we come out with something called team spirit. Without it a school limps along, at best. Students do too, in more ways than we care to admit. Worse, the finger-pointing and back-biting that thrive in the absence of team spirit are personally destructive to all of us.

With team spirit the whole school system is a functional unit. Better learning results because teachers are sharing the positives and negatives with one another in order to move toward a whole education for the whole child. That's why you must be constantly aware that it's our merging as a team that allows teachers to do together what they would never be able to do alone—and find greater fulfillment in the process. And remember, we are here as your colleagues to help you make your career in education everything you have ever wanted it to be. You are part of a team. We

53

welcome your membership and invite your participation to help give our children a quality education today and tomorrow and to enrich their lives.